★ IT'S MY STATE! ★

IDAHO

Doug Sanders

Jacqueline Laks Gorman

Cavendish Square

New York

Published in 2014 by Cavendish Square Publishing, LLC
303 Park Avenue South, Suite 1247, New York, NY 10010

Library of Congress Cataloging-in-Publication Data

Sanders, Doug, 1972-
      Idaho / Doug Sanders, Jacqueline Laks Gorman. — 2nd ed.
         p. cm. — (It's my state!)
      Summary: Surveys the history, geography, government, economy, and people of Idaho — Provided by publisher.
      Includes bibliographical references and index.
      ISBN 978-0-7614-7998-7 (hardcover) —ISBN 978-1-62712-099-9 (paperback) — ISBN 978-0-7614-8005-1 (ebook)
      1. Idaho—Juvenile literature. I. Gorman, Jacqueline Laks, 1955- II. Title.
   F746.3.S26 2014
   979.6—dc23
                                        2012024134

Second Edition developed for Cavendish Square Publishing by RJF Publishing LLC (www.RJFpublishing.com)
Series Designer, Second Edition: Tammy West/Westgraphix LLC

IDAHO

CONTENTS

State Bird: Mountain Bluebird

A member of the thrush family, the mountain bluebird was adopted as the state bird in 1931. Males tend to be pale sky blue, with darker patches on their backs. Females are blue-gray with a blue tail and wings. About 6 inches (15 centimeters) long, the mountain bluebird eats mostly insects. It will sometimes swoop down on its prey quickly from a tree limb.

State Tree: Western White Pine

The western white pine was adopted as the state tree in 1935. This stately tree reaches heights of 175 feet (55 meters). The trunk can grow to be 5 to 8 feet (1.5 to 2.5 m) wide. The world's largest western white pine stands near Elk River at a height of 219 feet (67 m). The largest remaining stand of these trees in the United States grows in northern Idaho.

State Flower: Syringa

Explorer Meriwether Lewis described this plant in his journal in the early 1800s. The plant has clusters of white flowers and grows like a bush. The shrubs can grow up to 10 feet (3 m) tall. American Indians used branches of the syringa to make bows, arrows, and cradles.

State Gem: Star Garnet

Star garnets are found almost only in Idaho, mainly in Benewah and Latah counties. These stones are similar to quartz and are usually purple. The star garnet was named the state gem in 1967.

State Fossil: Hagerman Horse Fossil

The oldest known relative of the modern horse, the Hagerman horse was adopted as the state fossil in 1988. About thirty complete skeletons and parts of two hundred other horses have been found at Idaho's Hagerman Fossil Beds National Monument.

State Fish: Cutthroat Trout

The cutthroat trout is native to Idaho and was studied and described by explorer William Clark. It gets its name from the red-orange stripe on its lower jaw. Its back is usually gray-green, with brown and yellow sides. It sometimes has patches of pink on its belly.

The Gem State

Idaho, located in the northwestern United States, was once described as "a vast sea of mountains." About eighty different mountain ranges rise across the state. Many of these ranges are part of the Rocky Mountains, which slash through the center of the state, making the region one of the most rugged areas in the United States. But in Idaho, for every high there is an equally impressive low. The chains of peaks and plateaus are broken by an endless spread of lush valleys, sweeping canyons, and steep gorges.

Idaho is also a land of water. Sparkling waterfalls, foaming rapids, and rushing streams feed the vast wooded areas that stretch toward the sun. Idahoans prize their millions of acres of unspoiled nature.

Idaho has a total area of 83,569 square miles (216,443 square kilometers) and a land area of 82,643 square miles (214,045 sq km). It is divided into forty-four counties. Boise, the state capital, is located in Ada County.

The state is changing. Throughout Idaho, cities are growing, and compared to the past, many people in Idaho are making a living in new and creative ways. But most residents believe the charm and special appeal of their home state will never change.

Quick Facts

IDAHO BORDERS

North	Canada
South	Nevada
	Utah
East	Wyoming
	Montana
West	Washington
	Oregon

Idaho is a land of mountains—and mountain lakes. Here, snow-capped peaks of the Sawtooth Range are reflected in Stanley Lake.

The Panhandle

Idaho is shaped roughly like a capital letter *L*. The narrow northern part of the state is called the Panhandle. This part of the state stretches straight toward Canada. It is a thin strip of land, only about 45 miles (70 kilometers) wide at the Canadian border. But what the region lacks in width it makes up for in variety. Lumber mills and silver mines dot the Panhandle. Idaho's Silver Valley is one of the largest silver-producing regions in the world.

The Panhandle is at the heart of Idaho's lake country. The area is home to a close grouping of lakes—more than can be found in any other Western state. From the shore of many of these sparkling gems, you can spot the bright sails of boats cruising past moss-covered giant cedars and jagged peaks. *National Geographic* magazine once called Lake Coeur d'Alene one of the five most beautiful lakes in the world. That is high praise for a lake whose beauty was once one of the best-kept secrets in the West. Lake Pend Oreille is even bigger than Lake Coeur d'Alene. It is the largest lake in Idaho, with an area of 94,720 acres (38,332 hectares), and is more than 1,000 feet (300 m) deep.

Considered "paradise" by explorers Meriwether Lewis and William Clark, who journeyed in the area in the early 1800s, the Panhandle is known for the roaring white water that rushes through the Lochsa, Clearwater, and other rivers. Float trips (often featuring large rafts) can lead to abandoned mines and ancient American Indian rock drawings.

The area is also home to the Seven Devils mountain range. These mountains, which are part of the Rockies, stretch north-south for 40 miles (65 km) along the Oregon border. Their tallest peaks loom some 9,000 feet (2,745 m) above the Snake River. The mountaintops are often covered with snow even into the summer. Those who brave the heights are rewarded with a spectacular sight. A climber can sit back and enjoy a sweeping view of four states: Idaho, Oregon, Washington, and Montana.

To the east, the dense green forests of the Bitterroot Mountains begin. They form much of the state's border with Montana. Northern Idaho is also the site of the deepest river gorge in the United States—Hells Canyon, which extends for about 50 miles (80 km) and in places is almost 8,000 feet (2,450 m) deep. The canyon walls are made of black, crumbly basalt, a type of rock. Hells Canyon was carved by the Snake River, which runs through it. The canyon is located on the border between Idaho and Oregon. The Snake River itself forms the actual border between the two states. Much of Hells Canyon and the surrounding wilderness are now part of the Hells Canyon National Recreation Area, which was established by the U.S. Congress in 1975.

Idaho Counties

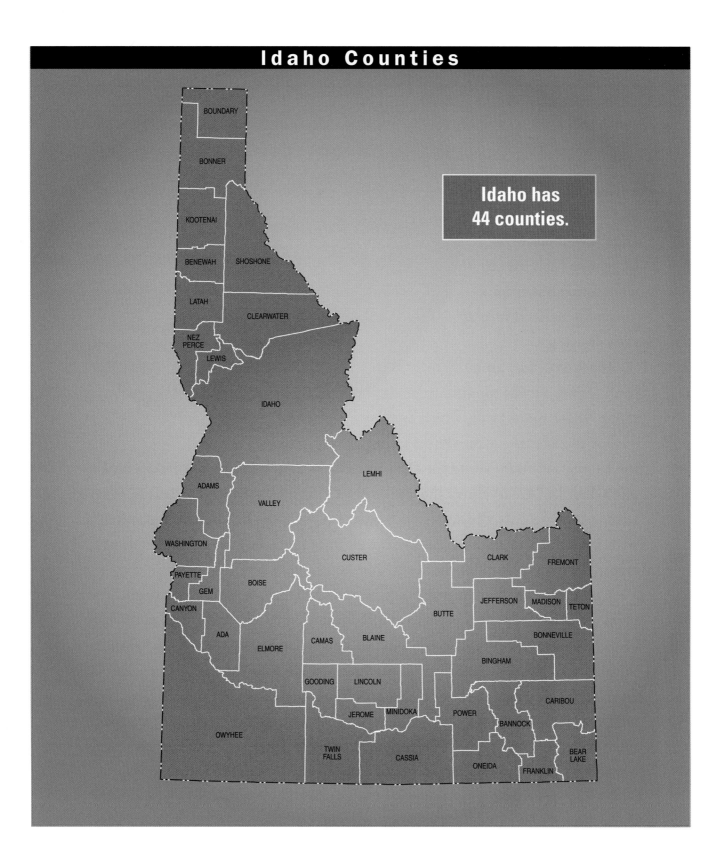

Idaho has
44 counties.

BOUNDARY

BONNER

KOOTENAI

BENEWAH

SHOSHONE

LATAH

CLEARWATER

NEZ
PERCE

LEWIS

IDAHO

LEMHI

ADAMS

VALLEY

WASHINGTON

CUSTER

CLARK

FREMONT

PAYETTE

BOISE

JEFFERSON

MADISON

TETON

GEM

CANYON

BUTTE

BONNEVILLE

ADA

CAMAS

BLAINE

ELMORE

BINGHAM

GOODING

LINCOLN

CARIBOU

JEROME

MINIDOKA

POWER

BANNOCK

OWYHEE

TWIN
FALLS

CASSIA

ONEIDA

FRANKLIN

BEAR
LAKE

The rolling, blue-flowered hills of the Palouse region, on the border with Washington, could be called the breadbasket of Idaho. Lentils, peas, and miles and miles of wheat grow in the region's dark, rich soils. Another of the many wonders of the Panhandle is the city of Lewiston. It is close to Idaho's western border and is actually a seaport, located where the Snake and Clearwater rivers meet. Ships travel 470 miles (755 km) from the Pacific Ocean—first up the Columbia River and then up the Snake River—to reach this bustling inland port.

Southwestern Idaho

Just like the Panhandle, southwestern Idaho is all about variety. Here, farm valleys are lined with cornrows and fields of alfalfa and mint. Southwestern Idaho is the site of many orchards and wineries. This region is also home to Boise, the state's largest city as well as its capital. Known as the City of Trees, Boise is framed by hills and mountains. Considered a Western gem, it is the urban heart of the state. You can stroll through the botanical gardens, visit a museum, or go to the zoo.

Fishing is a popular pastime for visitors to Idaho's many rivers and lakes.

Many people enjoy hiking in Bruneau Dunes State Park. To protect the dunes, no vehicles are allowed.

Heading an hour away from the city in almost any direction, you enter a completely different world. The region north of Boise is "classic" Idaho terrain. Clear-running streams, shimmering lakes, and steep, pine-covered slopes fight for your attention. This is a popular recreation area, where skiing and snowboarding are top draws in the winter. Some of Idaho's best fishing is found in the area, on Lakes Cascade and Payette.

Idaho's high-altitude desert country is to the south. It is laced with canyons made by creeks that often dry up in the hot summers. Bruneau Dunes State Park is famous for its dunes. It contains the tallest single-structure sand dunes in North America, at 470 feet (145 m).

In Their Own Words

My favorite place is the Stanley Basin area in the Sawtooth Mountains . . . where the salmon at Redfish Lake run red in the spring and early summer.

—Beverly Lucia of Mountain Home, Idaho

Central Idaho

This region is home to Sun Valley. Located on the edge of a dense wilderness, it is yet another of Idaho's recreational and scenic capitals. The Sawtooth Mountain Range—often called America's Alps—stretch nearby. They contain Mount Borah (also called Borah Peak), which at 12,662 feet

(3,859 m) is the highest point in the state. The range is at the heart of Idaho's central Rocky Mountains. More than forty peaks in the range rise to heights of over 10,000 feet (3,000 m). Thousands of beautiful alpine lakes are found in the range.

Central Idaho also includes the Snake River Plain. Millions of years ago, lava bubbled up through cracks in the Earth's surface. It hardened to form the plains along the Snake River. The plains here stretch for 20 to 40 miles (32 to 64 km) on each side of the Snake River as it flows toward the Oregon border. They offer some of Idaho's richest farmland. The river starts in Wyoming and twists and turns its way west through 570 miles (915 km) of Idaho. It is the state's lifeline, with several of Idaho's largest cities on or near the river.

Quick Facts

LOST AND UPSIDE DOWN RIVERS

Idaho's Big Lost River gets its name from the fact that it disappears for a stretch and flows underground. Another Idaho waterway, the Big Wood River, is sometimes called the upside down river. One section is about 100 feet (30 m) deep and 4 feet (1.2 m) wide, while a few miles downstream, the river becomes about 4 feet deep and 100 feet wide.

One of the longest rivers in the United States, the Snake River is more than 1,000 miles (1,600 km) long. Over half of the river's course is in Idaho.

The swift-flowing Salmon River passes through a federally protected wilderness area in central Idaho.

The prehistoric flood of Lake Bonneville (in Idaho, Utah, and Nevada) sent, at its peak, 15 million cubic feet (425,000 cubic meters) of water per second rushing down the Snake River. That is three times more than the flow of South America's massive Amazon River. The force of the water ripped open a wide canyon. True to its name, the Snake River Canyon snakes along, dotted with boulders and sheer walls that drop 530 feet (160 m) in some places. It is no surprise that this region draws white-water boaters, kayakers, and rafters.

The Salmon River, which flows across central Idaho and down through the eastern part of the state, was called the River of No Return by Lewis and Clark because it is hard to navigate upstream with its rapids and swift current. The Salmon is one of the few undammed waterways in the United States. It rushes through the Frank Church–River of No Return Wilderness, one of the largest such areas in the national wilderness preservation system. The rugged mountains and fir and pine forests here are filled with wildlife.

Eastern Idaho

Geological wonders are everywhere in eastern Idaho. The Soda Springs Geyser, for example, sends its column of water shooting more than 100 feet (30 m) straight into the air every hour. Eastern Idaho is also a great

Quick Facts

RANGES UPON RANGES
The southeastern part of Idaho is home to a number of mountain ranges. These include the Snake River Range, the Caribou Range, the Wasatch Range, and the Blackfoot Mountains.

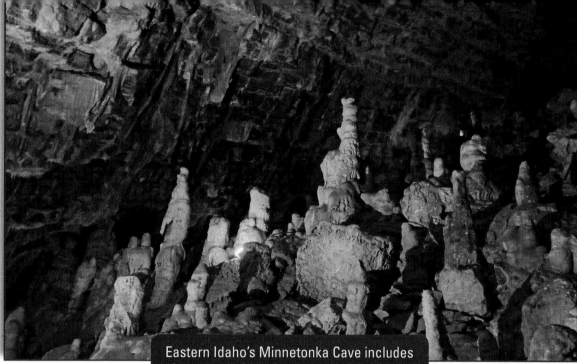

Eastern Idaho's Minnetonka Cave includes nine rooms of fascinating rock formations.

place to explore dark underground caverns. The Minnetonka Cave near Bear Lake is lined with ice crystals and bands of rock. It is rich with the fossils of plants and animals from prehistoric times. North of the town of American Falls is the Great Rift National Landmark, which includes King's Bowl, a crater 150 feet (45 m) deep that was formed by a violent ancient explosion. The area also contains the Crystal Ice Cave. The temperature in the cave is a constant 31 degrees Fahrenheit (–0.5 degrees Celsius), so the lake inside the cave is always frozen.

Those who like boating, fishing, and camping are drawn to vast Bear Lake, which is partly located in Utah. The shore of this lovely turquoise lake is lined with juniper and pine. Winter frosts here signal the start of the spawning run of the Bonneville cisco, a sardine-like whitefish found nowhere else in the world.

Sections of the plains are farmed in eastern Idaho. The land is covered with a patchwork of fields where potatoes and other important crops are grown. Rolling valleys lead to the snow-capped grandeur of the Grand Tetons. This range, part of the Rocky Mountains, runs north-south along the Idaho-Wyoming border. Tall pines and colorful quaking aspen trees make up the vast stretches of forest that rise in eastern Idaho. There are also lakes, rivers, and waterfalls throughout the region.

Eastern Idaho is also a great spot to ride in a dune buggy or off-road vehicle. The St. Anthony Sand Dunes cover an area of approximately 175 square miles (275 sq km). The dunes are made of quartz sand that built up over millions of years, carried by the wind blowing along the Snake River Plain. Many dunes are taller than those in California's Death Valley.

The dramatic landscape of Idaho's Craters of the Moon National Monument was created by volcanic eruptions thousands of years ago.

Climate

Idaho's climate varies from place to place and is influenced by weather patterns off the Pacific Ocean, which help to moderate extreme temperatures. In general, the northern part of the state is colder, wetter, and snowier than the south. In Boise—which is located in the southwest—the average low temperature in January is 21.6 °F (–5.8 °C), and the average high temperature in July is 90.2 °F (32.3 °C). Boise receives annual average precipitation of 12.1 inches (30.7 cm) and annual average snowfall of 21.3 inches (54.1 cm). In contrast, in Coeur d'Alene—located in the northern Panhandle—the average annual precipitation is 25.9 inches (65.8 cm), and the annual average snowfall is 52.2 inches (132.6 cm). The average low temperature in January in Coeur d'Alene is 23.3 °F (–4.8 °C), and the high temperature in July averages 85.4 °F (29.6 °C).

Idaho benefits from being fairly close to the Pacific Ocean. Moist warm winds sweep across the state from the west and help make the climate milder. In the winter, the state's wall of mountains in the east protects it from some of the cold winds coming from Canada and the Great Plains.

But as is true of any place, extremes are to be expected. At higher elevations in Idaho's many mountain ranges, snow can last until June. This has helped the

Snow cover that lasts well into spring in many of Idaho's mountain ranges helps make the state a popular destination for skiers and snowboarders.

state earn its reputation as a skier's paradise. In addition, when the snow melts in late spring, the resulting water is used to irrigate millions of acres of land.

Plants and Animals

With such varied terrain—and so much open space—it is not surprising that Idaho is home to a wide range of plants and animals. North of the Salmon River (which runs through the center of the state, dividing it into northern and southern parts), more than 80 percent of Idaho is covered in forests. By comparison, only about 30 percent of the region south of the Salmon River is wooded. Most of the state's trees are conifers, or cone-bearing softwoods. They thrive in the moist soils of the north and include Douglas fir, Engelmann spruce, hemlock, lodgepole pine, ponderosa pine, red cedar, western larch, white fir, and white pine. Hardwood trees include birch, cottonwood, willow, and aspen. There are thirteen national forests in Idaho.

Hearty grasses and shrubs that can bear the extremes of weather tend to be found in the drier south, but many types of shrubs and grasses grow throughout the state's mountains and valleys. Dogwood, elderberry, huckleberry, ocean spray, purple heather, snowberry, and thimbleberry send their roots deep into the soil. Idaho's wildflowers are often as colorful as their names. Fairy slippers, dogtooth violets, western springbeauty, Nuttall's larkspur, pussytoes, prairie

In Their Own Words

stars, buttercups, shooting stars, and Queen's cup brighten fields and mountain meadows, their blooms gently rocking in the breeze.

Idaho's wild animals make their homes throughout the mountains and plains. "You can drive for hours and see nothing but eagles, antelope, and coyotes," one longtime resident said. Idaho has one of the largest elk herds in the nation. Large mammals are drawn to the state's rich supply of food. White-tailed deer and mule deer feed on the grasses and other plants. Bighorn sheep can also be seen in different parts of the state. To the south, bison, the symbols of the plains, lumber along, grazing as they go. Some make very little progress between eating and sleeping. Although their numbers in Idaho are small—and decreasing—they are still a welcome sight.

Idaho is home to cougars that pad noiselessly over the rocky mountain slopes in search of a meal. The porcupine, however, is a poor choice for a meal. When threatened, it raises its sharp quills. Idaho also has large populations of raccoon, mink, muskrat, and otters. Most of these animals stay close to rivers, ponds,

Mule deer got their name because their large ears resemble those of a mule.

and streams. There are also grizzly bears, coyotes, wolves, foxes, and chipmunks.

Fishing is a popular sport in the state, and Idaho's waters are filled with many different types of fish. Steelhead trout and kokanee salmon wait for an unsuspecting insect to land nearby. Catfish, perch, bass, and crappie also swim through the state's waters.

The sounds of birds fill the skies over Idaho. Ringneck pheasants gather in grassy fields and underbrush, while red-billed chuckars and meadowlarks flit about. Waterbirds make their appearance, too. Ducks and geese gather on waterways, with their fuzzy young not far behind.

Idaho's birds of prey include the great gray owl, one of fourteen species, or types, of owls found in the state.

The Morley Nelson Snake River Birds of Prey National Conservation Area was established in 1993 to protect the environment supporting the densest population of nesting raptors, or birds of prey, in North America. More than seven hundred pairs of raptors nest there each spring, including prairie falcons, golden eagles, northern harriers, and American kestrels. The cliffs of the Snake River Canyon provide the perfect site for these birds to nest, and the nearby area provides small mammals for the birds to prey upon. Pesticides, drought, and wildfires have affected these bird populations, and their numbers have declined. Another problem is cheatgrass. This is a type of grass that is not native to the region but started to grow there. In some places, cheatgrass has taken over and forced out some of the native grasses. It is less nutritious than the native plants and dies sooner in the year. This leaves little food for some of the raptors' top prey: ground squirrels and rabbits. As a result, there are fewer squirrels and rabbits in the area, which in turn threatens the raptors. The conservation area established a resource management plan to protect the natural habitat and support native grasses there.

Plants & Animals

Harebell

The slender stalks of the harebell range from 8 to 20 inches (20 to 50 cm) long. At the end of each stalk hang delicate blue and purple blooms. These bell-shaped flowers appear from June to August and are found in valleys and on open hillsides and prairies.

Painted Turtle

This shy reptile can be identified by its colorful shell. Painted turtles live mostly in shallow bodies of water, but they lay their eggs on land. They have a varied diet. When young, they eat mostly beetles, maggots, and larvae. As adults, they eat snails, insects, crayfish, leeches, tadpoles, small fish, and many types of plants.

Huckleberry

The huckleberry is the state fruit, and several different species are native to Idaho. The plants are slow growers, often taking fifteen years to reach their full height. Their juicy purplish or black berries are a favorite food of bears, small mammals, and many humans.

Beaver

This large rodent can weigh up to 60 pounds (27 kilograms). With its strong legs and paddlelike tail, the beaver is a strong swimmer. It is also an excellent builder. It uses its teeth to cut down trees to create elaborate dams and warm, cone-shaped houses called lodges. The lodges are strong enough to protect the beavers inside from bear attacks, but they also have two escape tunnels for emergencies.

Moose

These large animals, which can weigh up to 1,500 pounds (680 kg), are the biggest mammals in Idaho. Male moose, which have large, flat antlers, can grow to be up to 7 feet (2 m) tall. They live off trees and shrubs—mostly maple and aspen—but will eat aquatic plants as well.

Mountain Goat

Mountain goats are not really goats. They are more closely related to antelope. Found most often in areas that receive a great deal of snow, these animals are highly skilled at moving about on rocky cliffsides.

From the Beginning

No one is sure exactly when people first came to the land now known as Idaho. There is evidence that around the year 11,500 BCE, small bands of people entered the area and decided to stay. They were Paleo-Indians, whose ancestors had walked across a land bridge that once connected Asia and Alaska. (Sea levels were lower many thousands of years ago. Because they are higher today, the land bridge no longer exists—it is under hundreds of feet of water.) The descendants of the first migrants spread south throughout the North American continent over thousands of years.

American Indian Peoples of Idaho

Over the centuries, a number of American Indian groups made their home in present-day Idaho. Life was not always easy for these early inhabitants. They learned to adapt to the land. There was plenty of food in the region's forests and streams, and several groups thrived in their homes in the mountains. The Coeur d'Alene, Pend d'Oreille, Kootenai, and Kalispel settled in the north. The Northern Paiute lived in the southwestern corner of the present-day state as well as in the neighboring region (what is now Oregon), while the Bannock and Shoshone dealt with the tough conditions in the desert country of the south.

These people moved about often, always in search of food. Fish was a major part of their diet, but they also hunted for birds and for small game. Women

This nineteenth-century photograph shows leaders of several American Indian groups.

gathered seeds and nuts. In the drier regions, the women dug the bulbs of the camas, a plant in the lily family that was an important part of the Indian diet.

Over time, the region saw the rise of two powerful nations—the Nez Perce and the Shoshone. They were the largest groups to settle in what is now Idaho. The Nez Perce lived mostly in the north-central portion of the present-day state, near the Salmon and Clearwater rivers. The Shoshone preferred the sagebrush country to the south. Horses (which had been brought to North America by Spanish explorers) were one of the reasons both groups became so strong. With them, the Indians could travel greater distances in search of food and could engage in trade. Horses also allowed them to hunt the bison (also called buffalo) that roamed the plains. The Nez Perce were skilled riders and became well known for their swift Appaloosas, spotted horses that the Indians bred in the rolling hills of the Palouse region.

American Indians in Idaho used horses for hunting bison and for traveling to trade with other groups.

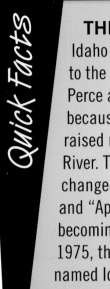

THE APPALOOSA
Idaho settlers referred to the horses of the Nez Perce as "Palouse horses" because the animals were raised near the Palouse River. The name then changed to "Palousey" and "Appalousey" before becoming "Appaloosa." In 1975, the Appaloosa was named Idaho's state horse.

These two leading groups grew to be rivals. They fought often. Parties of men clashed over the right to hunt bison or fish for salmon. Usually in the summer, though, the fighting stopped and different groups of Indians came together to meet and trade in peace.

Explorers and Fur Trappers

In August 1805, Meriwether Lewis and William Clark became the first white people to enter the land that is now Idaho. They were sent by President Thomas Jefferson to explore parts of the West that the U.S. government had recently purchased from France, as well as to look for a water route from the eastern United States to the Pacific Ocean. Lewis and Clark and their group passed through the region that now includes Idaho on their way to the Pacific. They entered the area by way of the Bitterroot Mountains at Lemhi Pass, along the border with present-day Montana. This is where they crossed the Continental Divide, the imaginary line that separates North America's river systems. (East of the divide, rivers flow toward the Atlantic and Gulf of

Mexico. West of the divide, they flow toward the Pacific.) Before them stretched miles of mountainous country that proved difficult to cross. The team of explorers was forced to head north and try crossing the Bitterroots at Lolo Pass. From there, they slowly pushed west.

Lewis and Clark were guided on their journey by a French-Canadian interpreter named Toussaint Charbonneau and his wife, Sacagawea. She was a Shoshone who had been born in the Bitterroot Mountains near present-day Salmon, then kidnapped by another group of Indians. She helped the expedition by identifying landmarks and easing tensions with Indians they encountered. One group of Shoshone who helped Lewis and Clark turned out to be led by her brother, whom she had not seen since her kidnapping.

With the help of groups of Shoshone and Nez Perce, Lewis and Clark were able to get through a September blizzard and travel west. The Indians guided them out of the Bitterroots. Lewis and Clark then built sturdy canoes and traveled down the Clearwater and Snake rivers. Leaving the region, they continued west on the Columbia River to the Pacific. They returned in 1806 and retrieved the horses they had left with the Nez Perce. They spent six weeks with the Nez Perce before continuing east to complete their journey.

The brave explorers proved to be the first of many. Their journals, maps, and stories helped attract others to the region. Fur trappers and traders, as well as

Help from American Indians was very important to the success of the Lewis and Clark Expedition. Indians gave the explorers horses and guided them through the Rocky Mountains.

missionaries, made their way into what is now Idaho during the following years. Canada's North West Company sent explorer David Thompson to scout the region for furs. He settled on the shores of Lake Pend Oreille. In 1809, he built a trading post called Kullyspell House. Although it did not last long, this first successful outpost proved to other non-Indians that it was possible to tame the wilds of the region.

The following year, the first U.S. settlers entered the area. Andrew Henry set out from Missouri and established Fort Henry, the first U.S. fur trading post in the region, near present-day St. Anthony. Soon, more and more people headed for the area, attracted by the rich resources of the West. Trappers decided to test their luck in the hopes of making a small fortune, mostly in beaver pelts. In addition, British companies, such as the Hudson's Bay Company, moved in. In 1834, two more trading posts were built in the area. Fort Hall (established by merchant Nathaniel Wyeth on the Snake River) and Fort Boise (built by the Hudson's Bay Company) helped draw even more attention to the region.

MAKING A TRAPPER'S POSSIBLES BAG

Trappers and other mountain men carried around items that were necessary for survival in the new land. These items were called possibles and included objects such as bullets, knives, a tin cup, and flint for starting fires. Most trappers and mountain men used possibles bags to carry these things.

WHAT YOU NEED

2 sheets of paper, each 8$\frac{1}{2}$ inches by 11 inches (22 cm by 28 cm)

Scissors

Cellophane tape or masking tape

1 piece of fabric, 14 inches by 24 inches (35 cm by 60 cm) (To make your bag look like a traditional one, you can use false suede, vinyl, or lightweight leather.)

Awl or sharp paper punch

1 piece of yarn, 4 feet (1.2 m) long

Beads with holes

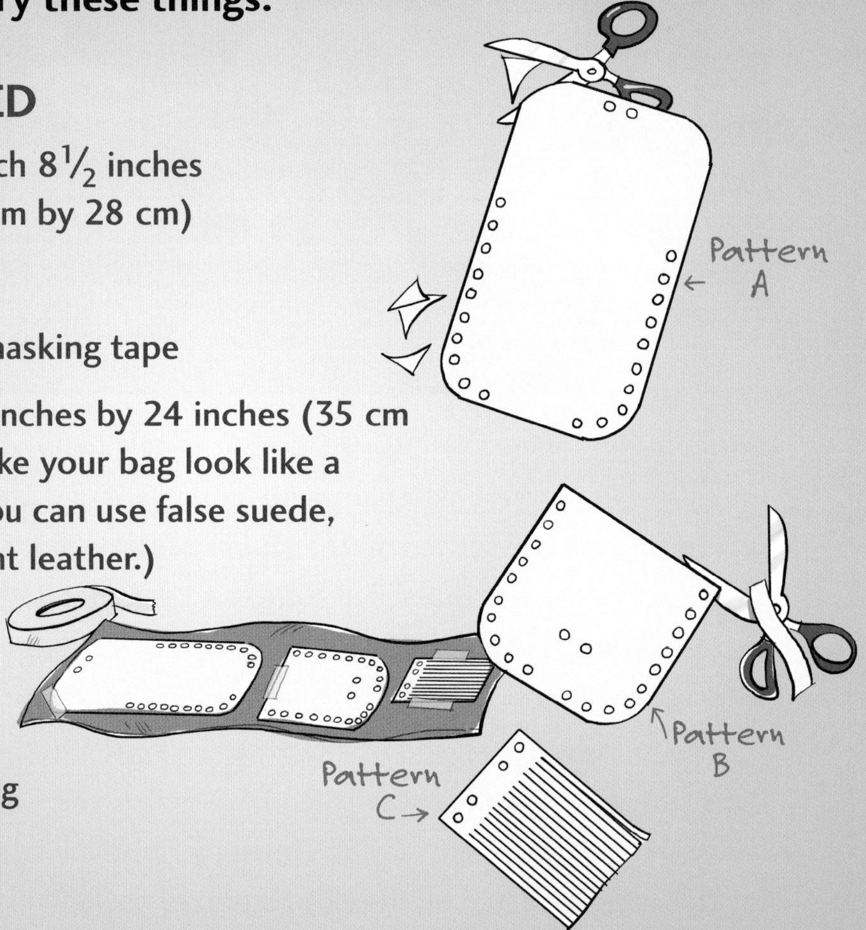

Pattern A

Pattern B

Pattern C

Make three patterns. Round all the corners of one sheet of paper using the scissors. This is pattern A. Cut the second sheet of paper in half. Take one of the halves and round off just two corners on the longer side. This is pattern B. Using the other half, cut a rectangle measuring 6 inches by 5$\frac{1}{2}$ inches (15 cm by 14 cm). This is pattern C.

Tape the patterns to the fabric using the cellophane tape or masking tape. Cut the fabric according to the patterns.

Following the diagram shown here, punch holes in the different pieces of fabric using the awl or paper punch. Ask an adult if you need help punching through the fabric. (If you are using an awl, you should ask an adult for help since awls can be sharp.)

On fabric piece C, cut fringes about 4 inches (10 cm) long.

Choose which side of your fabric will be the finished side. Lay the finished side of fabric piece A face-down on the table. Put fabric piece C (the fringe piece) at the bottom of A, finished side up, with the fringe hanging down. Be sure to line up the holes of A and C. Lay fabric piece B finished side up, over A and C, lining up the holes.

Thread the yarn in and out of the holes. When you reach the last hole, thread the yarn through the holes again, going in the opposite direction. When you get back to your starting point, tie a knot on the inside of the bag and trim off the extra yarn.

Fold piece A over to make a flap, lining up the center holes. Thread a short piece of yarn through the center holes in B and tie a knot on the inside. This should form a loop on the outside. Thread a longer strand of yarn through the center holes in A and knot it in place. The ends of this piece of yarn should hang down. These ends can be tied to the loop when you want to close your bag.

Tie on beads for decoration wherever you choose. Have an adult help you sew on a strap if you want to wear the bag over your shoulder. Now choose the "possibles" you need to carry, and have fun.

Missionaries and Settlers

In 1836, missionaries Henry and Eliza Spalding came to the area with a different plan in mind. They wanted to help establish the Christian religion on the frontier and to convert the American Indians to Christianity. Settling at Lapwei near present-day Lewiston, they quickly set to work. It was there that Henry Spalding printed the region's first book, established its first school, developed its first irrigation system, and grew its first potatoes. The Spaldings were among the first white people to establish close contact with Idaho's American Indians. Their work paved the way for other missionaries.

All this time, what would become the state of Idaho was not even called Idaho, nor was it officially a part of the United States. In 1846, as a result of an agreement between Great Britain and the United States, the United States gained control of what was known as the Oregon Country, which included all of present-day Idaho, Oregon, and Washington, as well as parts of Montana and Wyoming. (Before the 1846 agreement, the United States and Britain had both claimed the area.) The U.S. government established these lands as the Oregon Territory in 1848. Five years later, all of the land except Oregon became the Washington Territory.

During these years, many people came rolling through, hoping to start a new life in the Pacific Northwest. Families packed their belongings and, in most cases, parted from relatives and friends back in the East, never to see them again. Wagon trains made their way along the Oregon Trail, which passed through present-day Idaho along the Snake River Plain. Few of these pioneers were tempted to stay. After enduring the blazing heat of summer and the rugged terrain, many pioneers continued to travel westward for a more favorable location.

As many people from the East traveled to the Pacific Northwest in the mid-1800s, frontier towns sprang up in the region.

To Mormon settlers, though, present-day Idaho and nearby Utah to the south were a rough paradise. The Mormons, members of the Church of Jesus Christ of Latter-day Saints, came to the area seeking religious freedom and an end to the criticism and violence they often faced in the East and Midwest. Staking their claims in what is now eastern Idaho in the mid-1850s, hard-working Mormon farmers cleared fields and grew crops. They helped introduce irrigation to the West, an important method for watering crops in dry areas that is still used in the state today. They also built Fort Lemhi, adding another outpost to the frontier for a time. Most early Mormon settlers did not stay, but they were followed

In Their Own Words

There is plenty of good water for agriculture and manufacturing purposes, plenty of timber in the mountains, an abundance of grass for hay and pasturage in the valley, the lime and building stone abounds in all or most of the canyons. The soil is represented as being very good and the productions similar to the other valleys in this mountainous region....

—An 1860 newspaper description of the area that would become Franklin, at the time the Mormons were arriving

WHAT'S IN A NAME?

It is not clear exactly what the name Idaho means, if anything. The name—which was said to mean "gem of the mountains"—was originally suggested for Colorado in 1860. Three years later, it was officially given to the Idaho Territory. According to some historians, a member of Congress made up the name, thinking it sounded "Indian." Others believe a steamboat operator invented the name.

by another group of Mormons, who arrived in 1860. Members of this group founded the town of Franklin. It was the first permanent settlement in the present-day state.

Gold Fever

With the discovery of gold at Orofino Creek near the Clearwater River in 1860, present-day Idaho was no longer a place people wished to avoid. Miners, prospectors, and businesspeople flocked to the area in the hopes of striking it rich. Soon, other discoveries followed—gold near the Salmon River in 1861 and in the Boise River basin in 1862, and both gold and silver in the Owyhee River country in 1863. The news spread quickly. Small settlements—including Lewiston, Idaho City, and Boise—soon sprang up near the prime mining areas.

Present-day Idaho's population was growing. Eventually, there were enough people for the area to qualify as a separate territory, and local officials asked to be recognized by the federal government. On March 4, 1863, Congress created the Idaho Territory. Lewiston was named the capital of the large area, which included much of Montana and Wyoming. Within a few years, other territories were created, and the Idaho Territory included only present-day Idaho. Boise became the territorial capital in 1864.

The coming of the railroads brought even more changes to the new territory. Mostly, it brought people, who could now move about more easily and reach once remote places. The Utah Northern Railroad branched off into Idaho, reaching Franklin in 1874. The growth of silver and lead mines helped speed the laying of tracks in the north. By the mid-1880s, the Oregon Short Line railroad proved a valuable outlet to places farther west. Slowly, Idaho was becoming connected.

Indian Conflicts

The growing number of settlers and settlements brought conflicts with the area's American Indians. Eventually—sometimes by treaty, other times as a result of war—many Indian groups lost most of their lands and were forced onto reservations. Many of the Nez Perce, however, refused to go to a reservation. In June 1877, while a conference was taking place between the Nez Perce and the U.S. government, a group of Nez Perce killed four white settlers. This led to the Battle of White Bird Canyon, in which thirty-four U.S. soldiers were killed. Chief Joseph of the Nez Perce wanted to avoid further fighting. He also did not want to go to a reservation. He led his people toward Canada, taking a winding course through Idaho, Montana, and Wyoming. They engaged in

Gold was discovered in and around a number of rivers and streams in Idaho in the 1860s.

In Their Own Words

"I am tired of fighting. . . . It is cold, and we have no blankets. The little children are freezing to death. My people, some of them, have run away to the hills, and have no blankets, no food. . . . I am tired. My heart is sick and sad. From where the sun now stands I will fight no more forever."

—Chief Joseph, on surrendering to U.S. troops in October 1877

battles along the way with the U.S. troops pursing them, and although they were significantly outnumbered, the Indians avoided capture for months. Finally, in October 1877, the troops caught up with the Nez Perce, and Chief Joseph was forced to surrender.

Statehood

By the late 1800s, many people in Idaho wanted their territory to become a state. In 1889, in preparation for statehood, Idaho adopted its constitution. The next year, on July 3, 1890, the territory officially became the forty-third state. At the time, the Idaho population was 88,548.

Statehood came at a time when Idaho's economy was stronger than ever. A second mining boom had begun in 1882 with the discovery of more gold in the Panhandle. But it was silver that was to prove to be the area's true treasure. Lead became an important resource as well.

Despite the success of the mining industry, tensions were rising. Miners and mine owners disagreed over wages and working conditions, and the miners organized into unions. When the miners went on strike, the owners responded by hiring nonunion workers to keep the mines in operation. This only angered the miners all the more. In 1892, the area around Coeur d'Alene became the site of an all-out war after some miners used dynamite to blow up the Frisco Mine near Wallace. Martial law was declared by the governor. (Under martial law, regular law enforcement is suspended, and the military is used to enforce the law.) Federal troops were called in, and with their help, the violence was ended. Meanwhile, miners who were sent to jail formed a new union, the Western Federation of Miners (WFM), in 1893.

The conflict was to have far-reaching effects. Some miners never forgot the struggles of the early 1890s, and there were other violent confrontations in later years. In 1905, Frank Steunenberg, who had been the governor from 1897 to 1901, was killed by a bomb that was triggered when he opened his front gate. A member of the WFM, Harry Orchard, confessed to the crime, claiming that he had not acted alone. He stated that top union officials knew about the plot and helped plan the bombing. Their 1907 trial attracted worldwide attention. Famed lawyer Clarence Darrow defended the union officials. They were found not guilty. Orchard was found guilty, and he was sentenced to life in prison for his role in the murder.

The struggles showed how important the mining industry was to the state. The success of mining helped boost another part of the state's economy— agriculture. Farmers needed to raise food in order to feed the large number of miners. At the end of the century, ranching also grew. The spread of the

A parade in Boise on July 4, 1890, celebrates Idaho's becoming a state.

railroads meant ranchers could send meat to a wider range of places. However, conflict arose here as well, as sheep ranchers and cattle ranchers fought over who controlled the land their livestock grazed on.

The First Half of the Twentieth Century

In the early twentieth century, agriculture became even more vital to the state. Still, it was often hard to coax a living out of the land. "I am not encouraging the countrymen to come," wrote Josef Zpevacek to his relatives in Eastern Europe in 1905, "because the country side is not pleasant at all: it is very dry, trees are in the distance of 50 miles; summer temperatures reach up to 106." The state government decided to aid its farmers. Dams, reservoirs, and irrigation projects helped open more land to farming and ensure stronger harvests. Farms and ranches grew across the state.

When the United States entered World War I (1914–1918) in 1917, Idaho was ready. High demand for food around the United States meant the nation needed as many crops as the state's fields could provide. Idaho farmers borrowed money to upgrade and modernize their farms. After the war, when the demand for food dropped, the farmers had difficulties repaying the loans. Their problems continued during the Great Depression, a period of severe economic hard times that began in 1929 and continued in the 1930s. People throughout Idaho and the rest of the United States suffered during the Depression. Banks failed. Many people were out of work and scrambled to find a job, any job that would help feed their families. The federal government stepped in to help, setting up agencies to provide jobs. One agency, the Civilian Conservation Corps (CCC), employed thousands of people

Quick Facts

A GUIDE TO IDAHO
During the Depression, the federal government's Works Progress Administration hired authors around the country to write guidebooks about their states. Vardis Fisher, a well-known Idaho novelist, became director of Idaho's writer's project and wrote the state's guidebook. He also wrote other works of fiction and nonfiction about Idaho.

A loan from the federal government helped struggling Idaho farmers set up a sawmill in the 1930s.

in Idaho who set to work preserving and improving the state's forests, roads, and public lands.

Slowly, things improved. Idaho's first highway opened in 1938, connecting even more of the state's remote regions. World War II (1939–1945), which the United States entered in 1941, helped put an end to the hard times. Jobs were plentiful as factories produced supplies and arms needed on the battlegrounds of Asia and Europe. Once again, Idaho's farmers were called upon to feed thousands of hungry soldiers.

During World War II, when the United States was fighting against Japan, Idaho was part of a dark chapter in the nation's history. Japanese Americans were sent to internment camps across the West and Southwest. The U.S. government feared they would be disloyal to the nation or would work to harm the U.S. war effort. There was no evidence that Japanese Americans were disloyal. Nevertheless, more than 120,000 people were forced to leave their homes, jobs, and communities and were moved into these camps. One internment camp was Camp Minidoka in southern Idaho. Another was the Kooskia Internment Camp in the northern part of the state. In 1945, the people held in the camps were freed, but many found it hard to return to their normal lives. For many, their faith in America had been taken from them.

Boise and other Idaho cities have been growing rapidly in recent decades.

Recent Times

During the second half of the twentieth century, Idaho was influenced by many of the same shifts and trends that affected the rest of the nation. Manufacturing and other industries replaced farming as the main source of income. Cities and their suburbs grew as people moved from rural areas.

Idaho became an energy leader, harnessing the power of the atom. In December 1951, at the Idaho National Reactor Testing Station near Idaho Falls, nuclear power was used to create electricity for the first time anywhere in the world. In 1955, the nearby town of Arco became the first city in the world where the electricity was generated by nuclear power.

By the end of the twentieth century, mining had lost its hold as one of the state's most important industries. Logging, which had also been significant, likewise lessened in importance. New high-technology businesses cropped up in some of the state's urban centers, and tourism became increasingly important. Meanwhile, Idaho's population grew as people were attracted by new opportunities and the state's beauty. The state's population increased by almost 30 percent in the 1990s and by more than 20 percent between 2000 and 2010.

As Idaho continues to grow in the twenty-first century, should the state's lands be protected and conserved, or should certain areas and resources be developed to create much-needed jobs? Many Idahoans are working to strike a balance that makes sense for their state.

Important Dates

★ **11,500 BCE** Paleo-Indians first enter the region.

★ **1600s** Bannock, Coeur d'Alene, Kootenai, Kalispel, Nez Perce, Paiute, Pend d'Oreille, and Shoshone Indians live throughout present-day Idaho.

★ **1805** The Lewis and Clark Expedition enters Idaho at Lemhi Pass.

★ **1809** The Kullyspell House trading post near Lake Pend Oreille is the first structure built in the area by white people.

★ **1810** Fort Henry, the first U.S. fur trading post west of the Rockies, is built near St. Anthony.

★ **1834** Fort Boise and Fort Hall are established.

★ **1836** Henry and Eliza Spalding build the first mission in Idaho, at Lapwei near present-day Lewiston.

★ **1853** The Cataldo Mission is completed. It is the oldest building still standing in the state.

★ **1860** Gold is first discovered at Orofino Creek. Franklin, the state's first permanent town built by people of European descent, is established.

★ **1863** The Idaho Territory is created.

★ **1874** The railroad first comes to Idaho, reaching Franklin.

★ **1884** Rich silver deposits are found in the Coeur d'Alene Mountains.

★ **1890** On July 3, Idaho becomes the forty-third state.

★ **1904** Milner Dam brings irrigation to the south side of the Snake River.

★ **1951** Near Idaho Falls, electricity is produced for the first time using nuclear energy.

★ **1955** Arco becomes the first city in the world to receive all of its power from nuclear energy.

★ **1975** The Columbia-Snake Inland Waterway is finished, making Lewiston the farthest-inland seaport in the West.

★ **1992** Linda Copple Trout is the first woman to be appointed to Idaho's Supreme Court.

★ **2011** Idaho resumes management of the gray wolf population in the state after the animals are removed from the federal endangered species list.

The People

In 2000, a problem arose at the University of Idaho. The school was creating an advertisement to recruit future students. A graphic artist working for the university could not find an image in the university's archives that showed students of different races. He used computer software to change a photograph of a group of students so that it seemed as if it included an Asian-American and an African-American student. Many people were upset when they found out. Robert Hoover, then president of the university, hoped that no one was offended by the change. "I understand it was done in the interest of reflecting our commitment to diversity at the University of Idaho," he said. At the time, the university's student body was only 1 percent African American and 2 percent Asian. On the one hand, Idaho does have a mostly white population. According to the 2010 U.S. Census, 89.1 percent of the total population is white. On the other hand, diversity has always played a major role in shaping the state. Both in the past and in the present, Idaho has been home to a wide range of people. Today, Idaho has more than 1,567,000 people. Idahoans of different cultures and backgrounds live together in communities spread across the state.

Still, Idaho's population has changed through the centuries. In the days of Lewis and Clark, English was not yet spoken in Idaho. The two explorers met American Indians who spoke Spanish as well as the many Indian languages of the region. During the time of the fur trade, French Canadians introduced the

People from a variety of backgrounds
make up Idaho's population today.

Like many place names in Idaho, Boise's name comes from a French word.

French language to the area. They left their mark in the names of several places, including Boise, which means "wooded," and Coeur d'Alene, meaning "heart of the awl" (a tool used for drilling holes). Other groups also left traces of their presence in the state. Owyhee County in southwestern Idaho was named in honor of three Hawaiian Islanders who came to work in the trading posts there. Owyhee was an early spelling for "Hawaii." From 1834 to 1844, almost the entire staff of Fort Boise was from Hawaii.

The mining boom helped bring people from all over. Mexicans and Europeans, as well as African Americans and white people from elsewhere in the United States, all headed to Idaho. But most of the miners were Asian. By 1870, a majority of Idaho's miners were Chinese laborers. Few of them stayed after the decline of mining, but in the early days of the gold rush, these workers made up a quarter of the region's population. Many Idahoans today are descendants of settlers of English, Irish, and Scottish origin who came to the area from the East and the Midwest. Descendants of people of French,

Quick Facts

LARGEST CITIES
Boise is Idaho's largest city, with 205,671 people in 2010, according to the U.S. Census Bureau. Nampa was the second-largest city in 2010, with 81,557 people, followed by Meridian, with 75,092. Idaho Falls was fourth, with 56,813 people, followed closely by Pocatello, with 54,255 people.

Swiss, German, Czech, Polish, Slovak, and Scandinavian origin also add to the state's ethnic mix.

Hispanics

Today, as in many other U.S. states, Hispanic Americans make up the fastest-growing population group. In 2010, Hispanics (people who trace their origins to a Spanish-speaking culture) were more than 11 percent of Idaho's population. According to the U.S. Bureau of the Census, the number of Hispanic people in Idaho increased by 73 percent between 2000 and 2010. The greatest increase was seen in the Snake River Valley area.

Most of the Hispanic people in Idaho are of Mexican descent, but people who trace their origins to places all over the Spanish-speaking world have come to the state. People of Central American heritage, especially Guatemalan and Honduran backgrounds, are settling in the Treasure Valley area of southwestern Idaho. The state has even been called a Latino melting pot. Some Hispanic Americans have been living in Idaho for generations, and others have recently arrived.

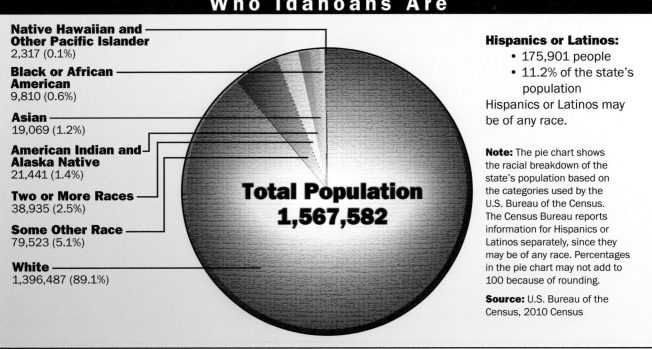

Who Idahoans Are

Native Hawaiian and Other Pacific Islander
2,317 (0.1%)

Black or African American
9,810 (0.6%)

Asian
19,069 (1.2%)

American Indian and Alaska Native
21,441 (1.4%)

Two or More Races
38,935 (2.5%)

Some Other Race
79,523 (5.1%)

White
1,396,487 (89.1%)

Total Population 1,567,582

Hispanics or Latinos:
- 175,901 people
- 11.2% of the state's population

Hispanics or Latinos may be of any race.

Note: The pie chart shows the racial breakdown of the state's population based on the categories used by the U.S. Bureau of the Census. The Census Bureau reports information for Hispanics or Latinos separately, since they may be of any race. Percentages in the pie chart may not add to 100 because of rounding.

Source: U.S. Bureau of the Census, 2010 Census

Hispanic Americans are Idaho's fastest-growing cultural group.

The Hispanic women's organization Mujeres Unidas de Idaho (United Women of Idaho) was once mostly made up of Mexican Americans.

Over the years, it has grown to include many members from other Hispanic backgrounds. Among its activities, Mujeres Unidas works to encourage Hispanic-American women to take leadership roles in their communities. Various Latino organizations in Idaho strive to help preserve traditions, as well as to raise awareness of and address issues that affect the Hispanic community. These issues include access to quality education and health care. Also, many newcomers arrive with limited knowledge of English. To help meet the needs of these people, businesses and government agencies are hiring more bilingual employees or offering their workers Spanish-language classes.

Basques

Beginning in the late 1800s, and especially between 1900 and 1920, a large number of Basque immigrants came to Idaho from the Pyrenees Mountains region of Spain and France. They worked mostly as sheepherders. The rugged country of Idaho was a logical choice for people who had left their mountain

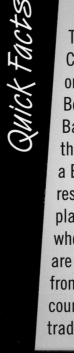

Quick Facts

THE BASQUE BLOCK
The Basque Museum and Cultural Center is located on Grove Street in downtown Boise, on what is called the Basque Block. In addition to the museum, the block has a Basque market, Basque restaurants, and a gathering place called the Basque Center, where traditional dances are practiced. There is also a fronton, or Basque handball court, where people play the traditional game of pala.

Children of Basque heritage perform a traditional dance at Boise's annual festival in honor of Saint Ignatius of Loyola.

homes back in Europe. The Basque newcomers thrived, and today, Boise has the largest Basque community in the United States. Each year at the end of July, a festival is held to honor Saint Ignatius of Loyola, the patron saint of the Basque homeland. There are sports and games, picnics, and church services. But usually the highlight of the festival is a display of Basque dances.

Boise is also home to the Basque Museum and Cultural Center. It honors the heritage of Basque residents in the area. The center's staff is proud of an ongoing project to preserve the oral history of the Basque communities in the American West. The museum's staff interviews and records the many different experiences of people of Basque heritage. The project helps preserve their stories and the stories of their ancestors before they are lost forever. Interviews that have already been conducted are being posted online at the museum's website.

American Indians

Approximately 21,000 American Indians live in Idaho today. They are spread across the state, in cities and towns as well as on Idaho's four reservations. The state's American Indians are citizens of Idaho, but they are also part of their own tribal communities. American Indians in Idaho today include people from groups such as the Nez Perce, Kootenai, Shoshone, Bannock, Coeur d'Alene, and Northern Paiute.

In eastern Idaho just north of Pocatello is the 521,500-acre (211,000-ha) Fort Hall Indian Reservation of the Shoshone and Bannock people. The reservation is just a small part of the land that these people roamed for thousands of years. The Coeur d'Alene Indian Reservation is located in the Panhandle. It is 598,500 acres (242,200 ha). The Duck Valley Reservation, which covers 288,000 acres (116,550 ha), is the home of the Shoshone and Paiute. This reservation lies on the state line between Idaho and Nevada. The Nez Perce Indian Reservation, in southwestern Idaho, covers 770,000 acres (311,600 ha).

Once, many people living on the reservations struggled to make ends meet. The reservations were often located far from developed areas, so residents had trouble finding jobs. But the tribal leaders have found a way around these challenges. They have created their own jobs and an even greater sense of independence. Income from agriculture, tourism, casinos, and the sale of native crafts helps provide the Indians with a better quality of life.

Historians have called the American Indians "the first environmentalists." That is certainly true of Idaho's Shoshone-Bannock. They believe that all things, including the land, rivers, and animals, have spirits. These spirits must live in harmony and balance with each other. Otherwise, they sicken and die. In defense of this belief, in recent years concerned Shoshone have spoken out about some of the abuses they see occurring around them. They have successfully challenged plans to build a high-level nuclear waste dump near what some politicians have called their "barren" homelands. They opposed the building of a dam that would threaten a site where healing rituals have taken place for generations. In 2010, they filed a lawsuit against some federal agencies to block a land deal with a

A dance competition is one of the events at the annual Shoshone-Bannock Festival.

private company because they said it could lead to greater air pollution. By working together, the Indians have helped preserve the land they cherish.

Amy Trice was a Kootenai Indian who died in 2011. She remembered the days when things were bleak for her people. By the 1930s, the Kootenai were a small band settled near Bonners Ferry in a small cluster of tepees. Most of the land that had been given to them by the U.S. Bureau of Indian Affairs had been taken away over the years until only a small parcel remained. Local activists managed to persuade the government to build eighteen houses, but they had no running water. More than forty years later, little had changed. The Bureau of Indian Affairs claimed the tribe was too small to receive any more assistance from the government. So Trice, then chairwoman of the Kootenai, and the rest of her band took a bold step. In 1974, they decided to declare war on the United States.

Of course, they were not exactly serious. The "war" was really an attempt to draw attention to their cause. As Trice recalled, "All we had was just a fly swatter. That was the strongest thing we had." Their plan worked. People saw the poor conditions in which the Kootenai had been forced to live. As a result of the "war," things began to change, and new houses and other facilities were built.

Famous Idahoans

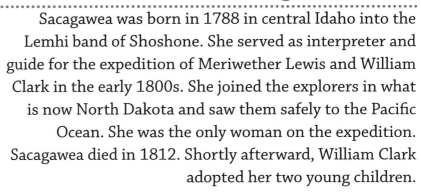

Sacagawea: Guide

Sacagawea was born in 1788 in central Idaho into the Lemhi band of Shoshone. She served as interpreter and guide for the expedition of Meriwether Lewis and William Clark in the early 1800s. She joined the explorers in what is now North Dakota and saw them safely to the Pacific Ocean. She was the only woman on the expedition. Sacagawea died in 1812. Shortly afterward, William Clark adopted her two young children.

Carol Ryrie Brink: Writer

Carol Ryrie Brink was born in 1895 in Moscow, Idaho, where her father was mayor. Her parents died when she was young, and she was raised by her grandmother. She attended the University of Idaho for three years before graduating from college in California. Brink became a writer of children's books, using the experiences of her family. Her most famous book, *Caddie Woodlawn*, was based on her grandmother's pioneer childhood. It won the American Library Association's Newbery Medal in 1936. Brink died in 1981. Brink Hall on the University of Idaho campus is named after her.

Ernest Hemingway: Novelist

Ernest Hemingway was born in Illinois in 1899. He traveled around the world as a journalist, leading an adventurous life. He first visited Sun Valley in 1939 and became a great fan of the area. He spent the last years of his life in Ketchum, where he died in 1961. Hemingway, who received the Nobel Prize for literature in 1954, was the author of such classics as *The Sun Also Rises, A Farewell to Arms, For Whom the Bell Tolls*, and *The Old Man and the Sea*.

Harmon Killebrew: Baseball Player

Harmon Killebrew was born in Payette in 1936. He was signed by the Washington Senators baseball team when he was just seventeen. Nicknamed the Killer, this power hitter was known for knocking balls clear out of the stadium. He later played for the Minnesota Twins and Kansas City Royals before retiring in 1975 with 573 career home runs. He was inducted into the Baseball Hall of Fame in 1984. Killebrew died in 2011.

Bill Fagerbakke: Actor

Bill Fagerbakke was born in California in 1957. He moved to Idaho and attended high school in Rupert and then the University of Idaho. He became an actor and had his first major success playing the assistant coach, Dauber, on the television series *Coach*. He also had a recurring role on the show *How I Met Your Mother*. Fagerbakke has done the voices of many animated characters, including Patrick Starr on *SpongeBob SquarePants*.

Picabo Street: Olympic Skier

This whiz on the slopes was born in 1971 in Triumph and was named after the nearby town of Picabo. She learned how to ski in Sun Valley and became a champion. In 1994, she won a silver medal in the downhill at the Winter Olympics. Four years later, she won an Olympic gold medal in the Super-G event. She also won back-to-back World Cup downhill titles in 1995 and 1996, becoming the first U.S. skier to win a World Cup season title.

Asian Americans

Few Asian Americans—only about 19,000—live in present-day Idaho. But during the gold rush days, a steady flow of Chinese laborers appeared in the state. Mostly men, they worked as miners or provided services to the industry by running restaurants and stores. By 1870, the Idaho Territory had 4,000 Chinese residents, about 29 percent of its total population. Later, Japanese immigrants arrived. Many Asian laborers found work on the railroads, either laying the tracks or helping to maintain the lines. They also farmed the fertile valleys.

Asian Americans have contributed to Idaho's growth and way of life since the 1800s.

Lewiston was one city with a strong Chinese presence. Most of the people who came there in the late 1800s were from the rural Toishan district of southern China's Guangdong Province. These immigrants brought their Taoist religion with them and practiced it at Lewiston's Beuk Aie Temple, which remained open until the late 1950s. Today, a museum at Lewiston's Lewis-Clark State College honors their heritage. It is part of an attempt to reclaim Idaho's Asian history.

Education

Idaho's first schools began teaching students years before statehood. Missionary Henry Spalding established the first school in Idaho, to educate Indian children, in 1837. In 1860, Mormons in Franklin established the first school to educate white children. Three years later, when the Idaho Territory was created, the first legislative assembly took steps to make sure that children in the region received an education. Legislators set up the position of territorial superintendent of public instruction. Then, in 1864, legislators adopted a school code that laid the basis for Idaho's public school system. By the end of 1865, Idaho had twelve schools educating 427 children.

In 2010, more than 281,000 students attended 435 public elementary schools and 232 public secondary schools in Idaho. Today, education is among the many state issues that are important to Idahoans, no matter what their race or background. Idahoans know that while some of their schools are successful, others face hard times and new challenges. During the first decade of the twenty-first century—a time of economic difficulty in Idaho and the rest of the United States—the state budget for Idaho schools was cut. This meant that students attended school for fewer days, went on fewer field trips, and had fewer chances to take classes in such areas as music and art. In 2011, Tom Luna, Idaho's superintendent of public instruction, introduced a reform program called Students Come First to improve the state's schools. One main part of the program was giving students greater access to technology. Every student, for example, would be provided with a laptop computer.

Idaho has three state universities. The University of Idaho, located in Moscow, is the oldest. It was founded by the territorial legislature in 1889. The university has more than 12,000 students and the only law school in Idaho. Boise State University, founded in Boise in 1932, is the largest university, with about 19,660 students. Idaho State University, in Pocatello, was founded in 1901 and has about 14,500 students.

Lewis-Clark State College, in Lewiston, is a four-year state college. In addition, Idaho has four two-year state colleges. There are also a number of private colleges and universities in the state, including Brigham Young University–Idaho, located in Rexburg.

Boise State is the only U.S. university where students have the opportunity to take a Basque studies program or get a master's degree in raptor biology.

Calendar of Events

★ McCall Winter Carnival

An ice sculpture contest is the highlight of this festival held on the frozen shores of Lake Payette in late January and early February. There are also fireworks, parades, beard and hairy-leg contests, and snowbike races.

★ Lionel Hampton Jazz Festival

Some of the world's best jazz musicians perform as well as offer workshops for students from elementary school through college at this popular annual event held at the University of Idaho in Moscow each February.

★ Cherry Festival

Each year in June, along the Payette River, the town of Emmett turns its attention to the annual cherry harvest. There are pie-eating and cherry pit–spitting contests, a pie bake-off, a parade, a carnival, a quilt show, a horseshoe-pitching competition, and square dancing, too.

★ National Oldtime Fiddlers' Contest and Festival

Hundreds of the nation's top fiddlers compete each June in Weiser. There are eight different categories divided by age, from small fry to seniors, as well as a category for "twin fiddlers" and a grand champion division for all ages. Judges choose the most fantastic fiddlers, who receive prize money.

★ Julyamsh Powwow

The Coeur d'Alene hold an annual celebration—described as the largest outdoor powwow in the Pacific Northwest—each July in Greyhound Park near Post Falls, along the banks of the Spokane River. There are traditional dances, art shows, a horse parade, and more.

★ Snake River Stampede

This top-rated rodeo kicks off every July in Nampa. Events include bronco riding, calf roping, steer wrestling, and barrel racing. There are also buckaroo breakfasts, a parade, and concerts.

★ Idaho International Dance and Music Festival

Since 1986, dancers and musicians from such countries as Peru, New Zealand, China, and Armenia have descended on Idaho each summer to perform and share a bit of their culture at the same time. The festival begins in Burley in late July, then continues in Rigby.

★ Shoshone-Bannock Festival

Held in August on the Fort Hall Indian Reservation, this event features a rodeo and a softball tournament, as well as traditional games, dances, and crafts.

★ Three Island Days

Each August, Idahoans in Glenns Ferry remember the pioneer days of the 1840s, when wagon trains crossed the Snake River along the Oregon Trail. Events—such as a mountain man competition, wagon rides, and pioneer games—are held in and around Three Island State Park.

★ Western Idaho Fair

Idaho's oldest and largest fair runs for ten days in August in Boise, the state capital. With carnival rides, exhibits, entertainment, and animal shows, the fair has been entertaining visitors since 1897.

★ Ketchum Wagon Days

Every Labor Day weekend, Ketchum honors the Old West and its mining past with the Big Hitch Parade, featuring wagons, horses, mules, cowboys, Indians, and mountain men.

★ Spud Day

The Idaho potato is given its day in Shelley every September. Events include a parade, a "spud tug," and a potato picking contest. Free baked potatoes are distributed to all comers.

4

How the Government Works

Several different levels of government work to serve the needs of the people of Idaho. The state government deals with matters affecting everybody who lives in the state. Local governments provide services for people in a certain area. Idaho also plays a role in the federal government. Its citizens can vote for president every four years, and like all of the fifty states, Idaho is represented in the U.S. Congress in Washington, D.C. Each state has two senators in the Senate. A state's population determines the number of members it has in the House of Representatives. States with larger populations have more members, while states with smaller populations have fewer members. Based on its population, Idaho has two representatives.

County and Other Local Government

On the local level, Idaho's forty-four counties are each divided into three districts. The voters in each district elect a commissioner, so that each county has three commissioners. Two commissioners

Idaho's Capitol building in Boise was completed in 1920.

The governor's official residence, outside Boise, is used for ceremonial events by the governor and other high-level members of the state government.

are elected to two-year terms, while the third serves for four years. The commissioners make up the highest level of county government. Voters in each county also elect other county officials, including a clerk, prosecuting attorney, treasurer, and sheriff. They each serve four-year terms. These people provide important services and are chosen by voters because of the skills and experience they bring to the job.

Most of Idaho's cities have a mayor-council system of government. In such a system, the city's voters elect a mayor, who is responsible for preparing the budget and appointing heads of departments, such as police and fire. Voters also elect members of the city council, who must approve the budget and make the city's laws. Some of Idaho's cities—including Lewiston, McCall, and Twin Falls— have a council-manager system of government, in which voters elect members of the city council. The council members are responsible for making city policies, passing laws, and hiring a trained city manager, who acts as the administrator and supervises government operations.

State Government

Boise has been Idaho's capital city since 1864. The state Capitol building and other state government offices are located there. Idaho's legislature meets in the state Capitol building, and the governor's office is in that building as well. The governor's official residence (also referred to as the Governor's House or Idaho House) is located on a hill north of Boise. It serves as the center of many state ceremonies, as well as the governor's social and political activities. The Governor's House was established as the official residence in 2009. It was donated to the state by J. R. and Esther Simplot, who formerly lived there. J. R. Simplot made a fortune in Idaho in the potato business.

Idaho's state government has three branches—the executive, legislative, and judicial branches—which work to make laws and make sure that the laws are obeyed and interpreted correctly. Idaho's constitution was adopted in 1889 and came into effect in 1890 when Idaho was granted statehood. The constitution describes the functions and powers of each branch of state government. Since

Quick Facts

BOISE'S GEOTHERMAL ENERGY

In 1892, Boise began using the first geothermal district heating system in the United States. Geothermal systems rely on very hot water located deep underground. Wells are dug to reach the water, which is then sent by pipes to where it is needed. Today, City Hall (right) and other government buildings in Boise, as well as many other homes and buildings in the downtown area, are heated with a geothermal heating system.

Branches of Government

EXECUTIVE ★ ★ ★ ★ ★ ★ ★ ★

The executive branch enforces state laws. This branch includes the governor, lieutenant governor, secretary of state, state treasurer, state controller, attorney general, and superintendent of public instruction. All are elected by Idaho voters to four-year terms. There is no limit to how many terms these people may serve. To make sure the state's business runs smoothly, the governor appoints the heads of different departments and the members of different boards and commissions.

LEGISLATIVE ★ ★ ★ ★ ★ ★ ★ ★

The Idaho legislature makes up the legislative branch. This branch makes state laws. Idaho's legislature is made up of two chambers, or parts—the state senate and the state house of representatives. There are thirty-five senators and seventy representatives. All are elected to two-year terms. There is no limit to how many terms a legislator can serve. Groups of legislators serve on various committees. They help examine many of the important matters that affect the people of the state, from education to the environment to agriculture.

JUDICIAL ★ ★ ★ ★ ★ ★ ★ ★

Idaho's supreme court is the highest court in the state. It has a chief justice and four associate justices who are elected by Idaho's voters to six-year terms. The supreme court is the supervisor of the entire state court system, establishing rules and policies. The court hears appeals of rulings made by the state's Public Utilities Commission and Industrial Accident Commission. The second-highest court in the state is the court of appeals, which is made up of four judges. When a case is decided in a lower court but the decision is appealed, it is this court that reviews the case to see if it was handled fairly and without error. Decisions by the court of appeals can be further appealed to the state supreme court. Idaho's lower-level courts, where most cases are initially argued, include district courts and trial courts.

1890, it has been amended (changed) more than one hundred times. The Idaho legislature may propose amendments to the state constitution. A convention called by the legislature may also propose amendments. Then, during elections, the state's voters must cast ballots to approve or reject proposed amendments.

Individuals in Idaho often have their own ideas about how their state can be improved and how things can be run better. Citizens are often the best source for suggestions that can make a positive difference. Under the state constitution, Idahoans have the power of referendum. This means that, during an election, they can approve or reject any act passed by the state legislature. In addition, they have the power of initiative. This means that they can propose new laws and pass them during elections, independent of the legislature.

How a Bill Becomes a Law

Although new laws can come directly from voters through the initiative process, most state laws come from the legislature. A proposed law, called a bill, goes through many steps in the legislature. Usually, a bill is proposed and introduced in either the senate or the house of representatives. Once the bill is introduced, the original bill and fifteen copies are given to the secretary of the senate or the chief clerk of the house. He or she assigns it a number. The bill is then read to

Quick Facts

LARRY ECHO HAWK
In 1990, Larry Echo Hawk was elected attorney general of Idaho. He was the first American Indian in U.S. history to hold that position in any state government. Echo Hawk, who is a Pawnee, was born in Wyoming in 1948. He served as Idaho's attorney general from 1991 to 1995. He also served in the Idaho legislature and taught law. From 2009 to 2012, he served as assistant secretary for Indian affairs in the U.S. Department of the Interior.

the senators or representatives, who refer (send) it to a committee for consideration. The members of the committee examine the bill more closely. They may conduct research on the topic of the bill. They may also hold hearings to receive opinions about the bill from experts on the subject, parties directly affected by the bill, and interested citizens. The committee can change the bill, and it decides whether the bill should move any further or not. Many bills never make it past the committee stage.

If a majority of the committee members supports the bill, it is read a second and third time in the senate or house, where all the members of the chamber can debate it, perhaps make changes to it, and vote on it. If the bill is passed by a majority vote of the members of the chamber where it was introduced, it is sent to the other chamber. There, it goes through the same process as in the first chamber. If the

Members of Idaho's house of representatives meet in the state Capitol to consider a proposed new law.

second chamber votes to pass the bill without changing it, it goes to the governor. But if the second chamber makes changes in the bill before passing it, the full membership of the other chamber must vote on the amended bill.

Once both chambers have passed the bill in the same form, it is sent to the governor to be signed. If the governor signs it, the bill will become law. However, if the governor disapproves of the bill, he or she can veto (reject) it and send it back to the legislature. Often, a bill that is vetoed does not become law. However, if two-thirds of the members of each chamber vote to pass the bill, it will become law despite the governor's disapproval. A measure that the governor has signed or one that the legislature has passed despite his or her veto is then sent to the secretary of state, who assigns it an official number. It is now "on the books"—a state law.

Making statewide policies for Idaho's public schools and their students is one of the important functions of state government.

Contacting Lawmakers

★ ★ ★ ★ ★ ★ ★ ★ ★ ★ ★ ★

If you are interested in learning more about Idaho's legislators, you can go to

http://www.legislature.idaho.gov/who'smylegislator.htm

There, you can click on an interactive map to find out who your state legislators are. Also, you can go to

http://www.legislature.idaho.gov/howtocontactlegislators.htm

There, you can find information about how to contact your state legislators by mail, e-mail, or phone.

Making a Living

Idaho's wealth of natural beauty is matched only by its wealth of natural resources. Mineral deposits line the state. The rich soil nourishes a range of crops, including barley, peas, and—of course—potatoes. Cattle and sheep graze the plains on farms and ranches large and small. These are the products and resources that have helped make Idaho strong. Today, however, they make up a much smaller part of the state's economy than they once did. In their place, other industries have gained a foothold in the state. The people of Idaho have had to embrace change as they assume new jobs and careers.

Agriculture

Soil is perhaps one of Idaho's most valuable resources. Several different types of rich and fertile soil are found in the state. In the north, after ancient glaciers retreated during the last Ice Age, they left behind a mixture of various substances that helped make the soil rich. This soil helped give rise to the sprawling forests found in the region. Along the Snake River Plain and in other prairie-like pockets of the state, the soils were formed by tiny pieces of

Quick Facts

PLENTIFUL POTATOES

Idaho produces more than thirty different varieties of potatoes. Sold throughout the United States and around the world, they are used for many different purposes, but 60 percent go into the making of French fries.

Hay is one of the state's leading agricultural products.

Workers & Industries

Industry	Number of People Working in That Industry	Percentage of All Workers Who Are Working in That Industry
Education and health care	147,288	21.6%
Wholesale and retail businesses	104,894	15.4%
Publishing, media, entertainment, hotels, and restaurants	71,213	10.4%
Professionals, scientists, and managers	70,696	10.4%
Manufacturing	68,179	10.0%
Construction	46,467	6.8%
Banking and finance, insurance, and real estate	39,436	5.8%
Farming, fishing, forestry, and mining	36,718	5.4%
Government	36,443	5.3%
Transportation and public utilities	32,757	4.8%
Other services	27,816	4.1%
Totals	**681,907**	**100%**

Notes: Figures above do not include people in the armed forces.
"Professionals" includes people such as doctors and lawyers.
Percentages may not add to 100 because of rounding.

Source: U.S. Bureau of the Census, 2010 estimates

Canola, used to make cooking oil, grows on the Idaho plains.

hardened lava and by a material called loess. Many of Idaho's mountain valleys are covered in alluvial soil, which is made up of substances carried by the state's rivers and streams. This great variety of soils means that many kinds of crops can thrive in different areas across the state.

About 25,000 farms and ranches cover approximately one-fourth of the state. Agriculture is mainly centered on the Snake River Plain. Farmers use the river to make Idaho one of the most irrigated states in the nation. Potatoes are by far the leading crop. Idaho is the top potato-producing state in the United States, accounting for one-third of the nation's potatoes. Hay and wheat also contribute to the state's wealth. Idaho is a top producer of sugar beets, barley, peas, and mint as well.

Quick Facts

FOR EVERY PERSON . . .
There are more cattle in Idaho than there are people. In 2012, there were some 2.2 million cattle and calves in the state, compared with fewer than 1.6 million people.

RECIPE FOR POTATO PANCAKES

Idaho is known for its potatoes. Idaho farmers produce more than 13 billion pounds (5.9 billion kg) of potatoes each year. By following these instructions, you can make a batch of tasty potato pancakes using delicious Idaho-grown spuds.

WHAT YOU NEED

4 medium-sized potatoes

$1/_2$ onion

2 tablespoons (15 grams) flour

1 egg

Salt

Pepper

Cooking oil

Wash and peel the potatoes. Shred or grate the potatoes into very thin strips. Have an adult help you, since graters or shredders can be sharp. Put the shredded potatoes in a large mixing bowl.

Chop the onion into very small pieces, and add them to the potatoes.

Put the flour and the egg into the bowl with the mixture. Add some salt and pepper. Stir the ingredients.

Pour a little cooking oil into a large frying pan or skillet. Heat the oil using medium heat. When the oil is hot, drop large spoonfuls of the potato batter into the pan. Using a spatula, flatten the pancakes. (Have an adult help you with the frying, since the hot oil may splatter.)

After about four minutes—or when the pancakes turn a golden brown color on the bottom—flip the pancakes over. Cook for another four minutes.

Serve the pancakes while they are still warm. Many people like to eat potato pancakes with sour cream or applesauce. Enjoy your treat.

J. R. SIMPLOT

J. R. Simplot was born in Iowa in 1909. He moved to Idaho when he was only two. Raised on a farm, he left school when he was a teenager and went into business on his own, growing potatoes. By the early 1940s, the Simplot Company had become the largest shipper of fresh potatoes in the United States. In the 1950s, the company created

and marketed the world's first commercially successful frozen French fries. Simplot also convinced McDonald's to use his frozen fries in its restaurants. Simplot died in 2008. His company continues to sell potatoes as well as many other products. Since 1979, it has also sponsored the Simplot Games, a leading high school track and field competition, held each year in Pocatello.

The central and southern plains of Idaho are home to the state's beef cattle industry. Dairy farms dot the Snake River Valley as well. Sheep are also raised. Milk and other dairy products, as well as wool, are important sources of agricultural income.

Mining and Timber

Idaho's mines are record holders, especially those in the Silver Valley region of northern Idaho. This area, around Coeur d'Alene, has one of the world's largest concentrations of silver. The Morning Star is one of the deepest mines in the United States, while Bunker Hill ranks as the nation's largest underground mine. The Sunshine Mine is the richest silver mine in the United States, producing more than 360 million ounces (10,200 metric tons) of silver during its history. The Coeur d'Alene area has survived labor disputes, blizzards, snow slides, and political disagreements to become one of the richest silver-mining districts in the world. Since the 1880s, the entire district has produced more than 1.1 billion ounces (31,185 t) of silver.

Heavy equipment lifts phosphate rock from an open pit mine.

Although a major product, silver is just part of the state's mineral wealth. There is gold in central and southern Idaho; lead, zinc, copper, and antimony in the north; and molybdenum in central Idaho. Other minerals produced include garnets, limestone, tungsten, clay, and cobalt. Although the north is an especially rich area, valuable mineral deposits are found throughout the state. Phosphate rock, which is used to make fertilizer, comes from Idaho's southeastern corner.

Above ground, the state is graced with valuable resources as well. Forests cover about two-fifths of the state. Idaho is known for its cone-bearing evergreen trees. These include Douglas fir, Engelmann spruce, hemlock, lodgepole pine, red cedar, western larch, white fir, and white pine. But deciduous trees, which lose their leaves in winter, blanket parts of the state as well. Birch, cottonwood, and aspen line rivers and cover the hillsides.

Idaho is the eighth-largest lumber-producing state in the United States. Forest products companies operate in many Idaho counties. The state's forest products industry produces more than $1.8 billion worth of wood and paper products each year. Boise Cascade, a major manufacturer of wood products and building materials, has its headquarters in Boise.

Manufacturing

In recent years, manufacturing has grown to become an important part of Idaho's economy. This is not surprising, given the state's fertile fields, rich mines, and dense forests. These natural resources form the raw materials from which countless products are made. Food processing is a major Idaho industry, especially potato processing. There are also dairies, meat-packing plants, and businesses that process sugar beets and wheat.

The electronics industry has proved to be big business for the Gem State. Computer and electronic products now make up the state's largest category of manufactured goods. Idaho factories also create metal and wood products, machinery, plastic and rubber products, and chemicals.

All this activity accounts for 11 percent of the gross state product, the total amount of goods and services produced in the state each year. Some $6.2 billion worth of products were made in Idaho in 2010. They were shipped across the state, throughout the country, and around the world.

A factory in Caldwell manufactures tortillas.

Products & Resources

Potatoes

Idaho is potatoes. Spuds, as they are sometimes called, have long been a symbol of the state. Idaho produces more than 30 percent of the nation's potatoes. They generate more than $4 billion in revenue each year.

Tourism

Those who love to ski, fish, hike, or simply stare at the beautiful landscape rarely fail to find something to delight them in Idaho. The state has seven national parks, national monuments, and national historic sites and eleven national natural landmarks.

Wood and Paper Products

Idaho's timber is mainly softwood lumber. In 2010, more than $1.5 billion was made from the sale of Idaho's major wood and paper products. These include wood for construction as well as pulp, paper, tissues, and wooden matches.

Gold

Silver is king in Idaho, but gold mining continues to grow in the state. According to the U.S. Bureau of Mines, Idaho has more mineable gold than any other state. Many older mines have been reopened in recent years.

Cattle

In 2012, there were 2.2 million head of cattle and calves (including 574,000 dairy cows) in Idaho. July is "Idaho Beef Month," an annual event celebrating the state's beef industry and promoting knowledge of beef's nutritional value and economic contributions to Idaho.

Computer Chips

High-technology industries are relative newcomers to Idaho, but they have provided a new source of jobs, mostly in the state's urban centers. Micron Technology, a leading manufacturer of computer memory chips and other computer components, is based in Boise.

Services

While manufacturing is important to Idaho, the state's many service industries are even more significant. Teachers, librarians, restaurant and retail workers, bankers, lawyers, doctors and nurses, and real-estate agents are just some of the service-industry positions Idahoans fill. Most service jobs are found in and around the state's cities and large towns, but certainly not all. Forest rangers, rural shopkeepers, livestock veterinarians, and vendors of farm equipment and supplies all pursue their trades often far from the beaten path.

White-water rafting is one of the many exciting outdoor activities that bring people to Idaho.

Tourism is an important source of income for the state. The tourist industry brings in almost $3 billion a year and provides jobs for 26,000 people. More than 20 million people visit Idaho each year. Some come to hike in the wilderness, ski in Sun Valley, and ride the rapids on the Salmon River. Others come to trace the steps of pioneers and miners from long ago. Still others come to marvel at the state's many beautiful sights, including the Clearwater National Forest, Bruneau Dunes State Park, Craters of the Moon National Monument, Hell's Canyon, and Shoshone Falls.

The Two Idahoes

In many ways, there are two Idahoes today, one that is urban (with the people living in and around cities) and one that is more rural. One of the major shifts the state has faced in the past one hundred years or so is where its residents choose to live. In 1900, 6 percent of Idaho's population lived in cities. By 2010, that proportion had climbed to more than 65 percent. Census figures indicated that between 2000 and 2010, 80 percent of Idaho's population growth came in

SPEEDING UP THE INTERNET

According to a 2011 study, Idaho had the slowest Internet speeds in the United States for residential customers who were downloading such things as games and music files. Pocatello had the slowest speeds of any U.S. city. In addition, the federal government reported that Idaho was among the states where the difference in Internet speed between urban and rural areas was the greatest. A number of federal projects were under way in Idaho to improve high-speed Internet access.

its eleven metropolitan counties. As a result, some small towns are shrinking. They offer little to lure young people, who often have to look elsewhere to find good-paying jobs.

The state's "Old West" economy, based on timber, mining, and agriculture, is losing ground. Stiff competition from other states and nations, lower prices for some commodities, and the rapid shift in technology are just a few of the reasons. While one way of life is slowly fading, another has emerged to replace it. The "New West" economy has turned to high-tech industries and tourism to create jobs.

The gap between rich and poor in Idaho, which often reflects the two—urban and rural—Idahoes, has grown wider. On average, Idahoans who live in urban areas earn more than those who live in rural areas. In addition, in 2010, the poverty rate of rural Idahoans was 16.9 percent, compared to 15.3 percent for urban Idahoans. The message is that rural communities need to change their economies. They need to find new directions and explore new paths. The state government established the Idaho Rural Partnership, drawing upon both public and private resources, to strengthen rural Idaho communities and improve life there. The Partnership's Community Review Program provides rural communities with information that helps areas create action plans, so that they can grow and change in the way they want, enabling them to preserve their history and culture while still moving forward.

State Flag & Seal

The Idaho flag is dark blue with the state seal in the middle. A red scroll reading "State of Idaho" is beneath the seal. The flag was adopted by the state legislature in 1907. Since there were different versions of the state seal, the flag was readopted with the present portrayal of the seal in 1957.

The state seal was created in 1890 and adopted in 1891 as the first act of the Idaho legislature. It shows a woman at the left holding the scales of justice. She stands for equality. The miner at the right represents the importance of mining to the state. The elk's head in the center stands for Idaho's wildlife, the pine tree for its forests, and the grain and fruits on the bottom for the state's farming industry. The seal was designed by Emma Edwards Green. She is the only woman to design a state seal in the United States. In 1957, the seal was updated and streamlined by Paul B. Evans.

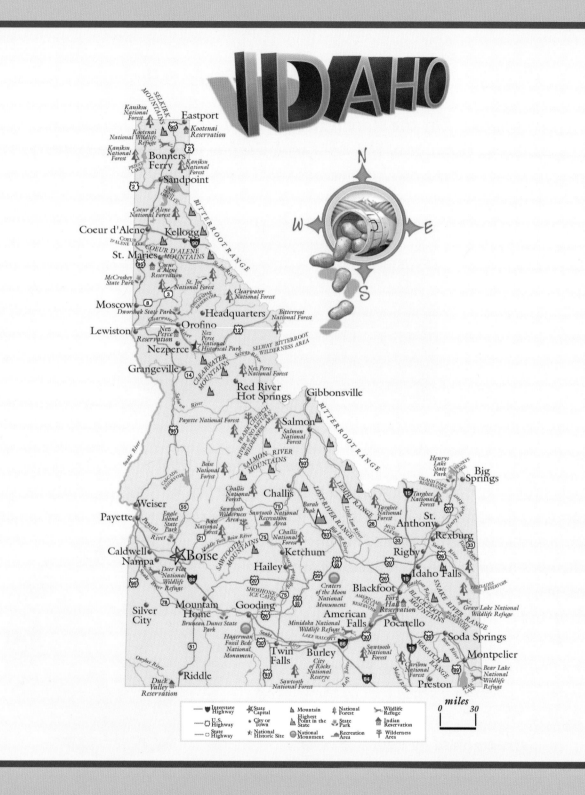

IDAHO

Selkirk Mountains
Kaniksu National Forest
Eastport
Kootenai Reservation
Kootenai National Wildlife Refuge
Kaniksu National Forest
Bonners Ferry
Kaniksu National Forest
PRIEST LAKE
Sandpoint
LAKE PEND OREILLE
Coeur d'Alene National Forest
Coeur d'Alene
COEUR D'ALENE LAKE
Kellogg
COEUR D'ALENE MOUNTAINS
St. Maries
McCroskey State Park
Coeur d'Alene Reservation
St. Joe National Forest
St. Joe River
Moscow
Dworshak State Park
DWORSHAK RESERVOIR
Clearwater National Forest
Headquarters
Bitterroot National Forest
Orofino
Clearwater River
Lewiston
Nez Perce Reservation
Nez Perce National Historical Park
Nezperce
SELWAY BITTERROOT WILDERNESS AREA
Selway River
Grangeville
CLEARWATER MOUNTAINS
Nez Perce National Forest
Salmon River
Red River Hot Springs
Gibbonsville
BITTERROOT RANGE
Payette National Forest
FRANK CHURCH RIVER OF NO RETURN WILDERNESS AREA
Salmon
Salmon National Forest
Boise National Forest
SALMON RIVER MOUNTAINS
Henrys Lake State Park
HENRYS LAKE
Big Springs
ISLAND PARK RESERVOIR
Targhee National Forest
Weiser
Challis National Forest
Challis
Sawtooth Wilderness Area
Borah Peak
LOST RIVER RANGE
LEMHI RANGE
Little Lost River
Targhee National Forest
St. Anthony
MUD LAKE
Rexburg
Payette
CASCADE RESERVOIR
Eagle Island State Park
Sawtooth National Recreation Area
Challis National Forest
Big Lost River
Caldwell
Nampa
Boise
Middle Fork Boise River
SAWTOOTH MOUNTAINS
Ketchum
Hailey
Big Wood River
Rigby
Snake River
Idaho Falls
Deer Flat National Wildlife Refuge
Snake River
SHOSHONE ICE CAVES
Craters of the Moon National Monument
Blackfoot
Fort Hall Reservation
BLACKFOOT MOUNTAINS
SNAKE RIVER RANGE
PALISADES RESERVOIR
Grays Lake National Wildlife Refuge
Silver City
Mountain Home
Bruneau Dunes State Park
Gooding
AMERICAN FALLS RESERVOIR
American Falls
Minidoka National Wildlife Refuge
LAKE WALCOTT
Pocatello
Soda Springs
WASATCH RANGE
Bear River
Montpelier
Owyhee River
Hagerman Fossil Beds National Monument
Snake River
Twin Falls
Burley
City of Rocks National Reserve
Sawtooth National Forest
Caribou National Forest
BEAR LAKE
Bear Lake National Wildlife Refuge
Riddle
Duck Valley Reservation
Raft River
Sawtooth National Forest
Preston

miles
0   30

Interstate Highway
U.S. Highway
State Highway
State Capital
City or Town
National Historic Site
Mountain
Highest Point in the State
National Monument
National Forest
State Park
Recreation Area
Wildlife Refuge
Indian Reservation
Wilderness Area

State Song

Here We Have Idaho

words by Albert Tompkins and McKinley Helm
music by Sallie Hume-Douglas

BOOKS

Bolen, Robert D. *American Indian Tribes of Idaho*. Boise, ID: Fort Boise Publishing, 2010.

Grey, Alan E. *The Life of Chief Joseph*. Idaho Falls, ID: Wasatch Press, 2008.

Lusted, Marcia Amidon. *Idaho: The Gem State*. New York: PowerKids Press, 2010.

Miller, Amy. *Idaho*. New York: Children's Press, 2009.

Otter, Lori. *Ida Tours the 44: A Book of Idaho's Counties*. Boise: Boise State University, 2010.

Stanley, John. *Idaho Past and Present*. New York: Rosen Central, 2010.

WEBSITES

Idaho's Official State Website:
http://www.state.id.us

State of Idaho Kids' Page:
http://idaho.gov/education/kids.html

Idaho State Historical Society:
http://www.history.idaho.gov

Visit Idaho:
http://www.visitidaho.org

Doug Sanders is a writer and editor who lives in New York. He is also the author of five other titles in the *It's My State!* series.

Jacqueline Laks Gorman has been a writer and editor for approximately thirty years. She was raised in New York and moved to the Midwest in the 1990s. She and her family live in DeKalb, Illinois.

★ INDEX ★

Page numbers in **boldface** are illustrations.